J

W9-CTI-493

What's LOVE?

by Shelley Rotner and Deborah Carlin
photographs by Shelley Rotner

CAPSTONE PRESS
a capstone imprint

Love is as **big** as the sun ...

3

and as **wide** as

a **summer** sky.

Love
opens our
hearts.

It makes us giggle and sometimes cry.

Love lets us **share**.

Love helps us
trust.

We love the animals that live with us

and those that are wild and free.

We love the
people in our lives.

We love our **families** ...

and our
friends.

We love our **neighbors**

and our **teachers.**

We love **ourselves.**

We love the feel of our **bodies** moving.

We love the **art** we make.

We love the **music** we play.

We love the **buzz** of **ideas** and **stories** in our heads.

We love the **colors** and **shapes** in the world around us.

Love brings us **joy** like
the first spring flowers.

Love **comforts** us like a strong old tree.

Love is a **gift** from me to you
and from you to me.

What do **you** love?

A+ Books are published by Capstone Press,
1710 Roe Crest Drive, North Mankato, Minnesota 56003.
www.capstonepub.com

Library of Congress Cataloging-in-Publication Data
Cataloging-in-publication information is on file with the Library of Congress.
ISBN 978-1-62065-069-1 (library binding)
ISBN 978-1-62065-756-0 (paperback)
ISBN 978-1-4765-1349-2 (ebook PDF)

Editorial Credits
Jill Kalz, editor; Heidi Thompson, designer; Wanda Winch, media researcher; Jennifer Walker, production specialist

Internet Sites

FactHound offers a safe, fun way to find Internet sites
related to this book. All of the sites on FactHound have
been researched by our staff.

Here's all you do:

Visit *www.facthound.com*

Type in this code: 9781620650691

Look for all the books in the series:

Different Kinds of Good-byes

Feeling Thankful

We All Do Something Well

What's Love?

Super-cool stuff!

Check out projects, games and lots more at
www.capstonekids.com

Printed in the United States of America in North Mankato, Minnesota.
092012   006933CGS13